Alfred's Basic Piano Library

Solo Book • Level 3

P *i a★ r o

TOP HITS!

Selected and Edited by E. L. Lancaster & Morton Manus

This series answers the often expressed need for a variety of supplementary material in many different popular styles. What could be more fun for a young student than to play the music that everybody knows and loves? The remarkable part of this *Top Hits* series is that soon after beginning piano study, young students can play attractive versions of the best-known music of today.

This book is correlated page-by-page with Lesson Book 3 of Alfred's Basic Piano Library; pieces should be assigned based on the instructions in the upper-right corner of each title page of *Top Hits.*

Since the melodies and rhythms of popular music do not always lend themselves to precise grading, you may find that these pieces are sometimes a little more difficult than the corresponding pages in the Lesson Book. The teacher's judgment is the most important factor in deciding when to begin each title.

When the books in the *Top Hits* series are assigned in conjunction with the Lesson Books, these appealing pieces reinforce new concepts as they are introduced. In addition, the motivation the music provides could not be better. The emotional satisfaction students receive from mastering each popular song increases their enthusiasm to begin the next one. With the popular music available in the *Top Hits* series (Levels 1A–6), the use of all seven books will significantly increase student interest in piano study to successively higher levels.

Published by

HAL•LEONARD®
CORPORATION

ISBN 0-7390-0298-8 (Book)
ISBN 0-7390-2117-6 (Book and CD)
All Rights Reserved. Produced in USA.

Distributed by
Alfred Music

Cover photos: Camera, popcorn box © 1999 PhotoDisc, Inc.
Backgrounds, movie clapboard © Eyewire, Inc.

The Unbirthday Song

from Walt Disney's ALICE IN WONDERLAND

Use with Alfred's Basic Piano Library,
LESSON BOOK 3, after page 3
(or with LESSON BOOK
Complete Levels 2 & 3, after page 41).

Words and Music by
Mack David, Al Hoffman and Jerry Livingston
Arr. by George Peter Tingley

Brightly

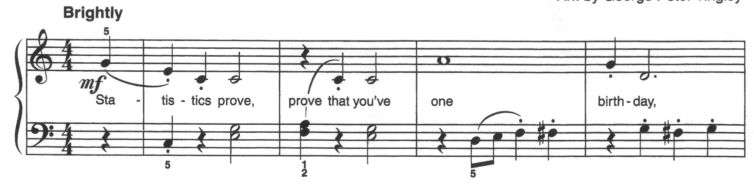

Sta - tis - tics prove, prove that you've one birth - day,

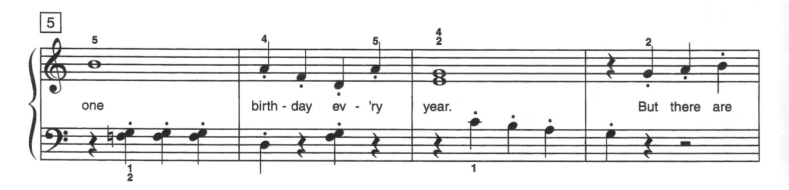

one birth - day ev - 'ry year. But there are

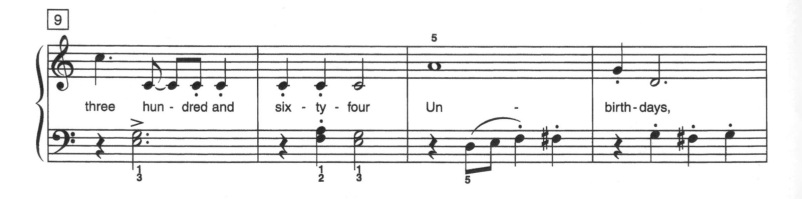

three hun - dred and six - ty - four Un - birth - days,

that is why we're gath - ered here to cheer. A

3

Use after page 11 (43).

I Just Can't Wait to Be King

from Walt Disney Pictures' THE LION KING

Music by Elton John
Lyrics by Tim Rice
Arr. by Sharon Aaronson

Happily, with rhythm

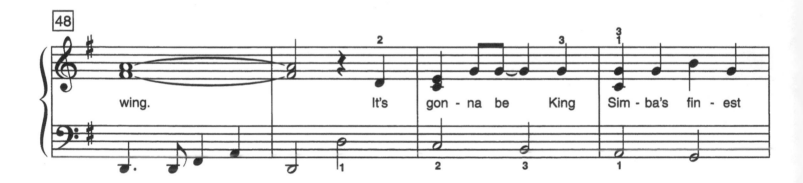

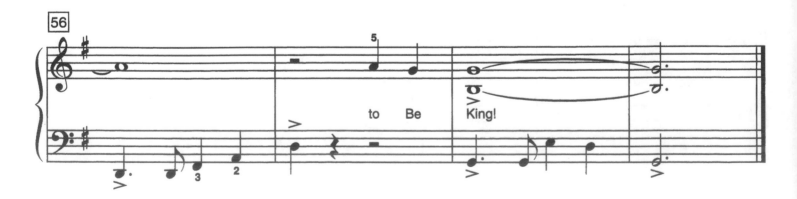

Rockin' Robin

Words and Music by J. Thomas
Arr. by Christine H. Barden

*Optional: Play eighth notes a bit unevenly,
in a "lilting" style: long short long short, *etc.*

**Play grace note exactly on beat 3 with the left-hand note and quickly move to the main note.

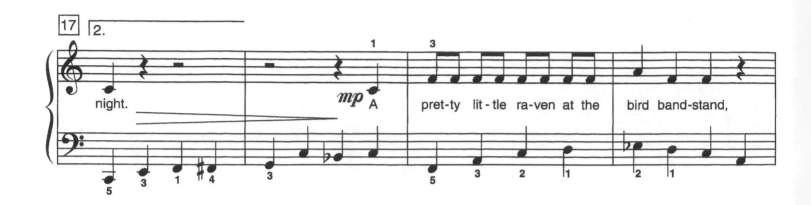

night.

mp A pret-ty lit-tle ra-ven at the bird band-stand,

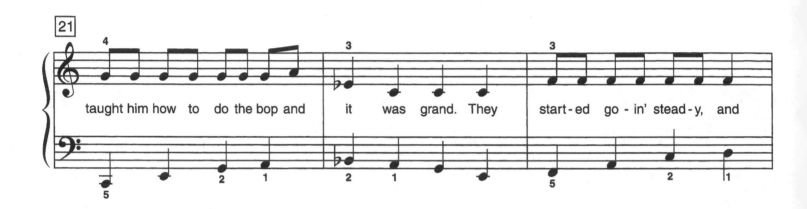

taught him how to do the bop and it was grand. They start-ed go-in' stead-y, and

bless my soul, he out-bopped the buz-zard and the o - ri - ole. *mf* He

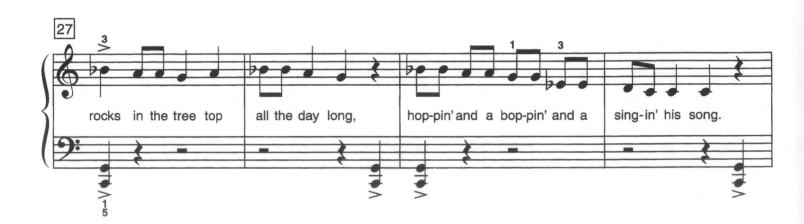

rocks in the tree top all the day long, hop-pin' and a bop-pin' and a sing-in' his song.

All the lit-tle birds on Jay-bird Street, love to hear the rob-in go

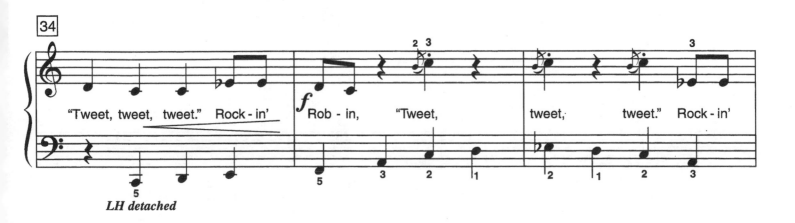

"Tweet, tweet, tweet." Rock-in' Rob-in, "Tweet, tweet, tweet." Rock-in'

LH detached

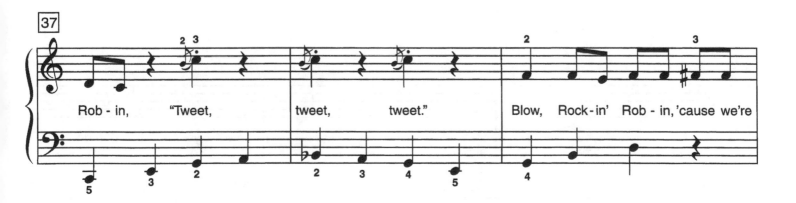

Rob-in, "Tweet, tweet, tweet." Blow, Rock-in' Rob-in, 'cause we're

real-ly gon-na rock to - night!

Use after page 19 (49).

My Heart Will Go On (Love Theme from 'Titanic')

from the Paramount and Twentieth Century Fox Motion Picture TITANIC

Music by James Horner
Lyric by Will Jennings
Arr. by George Peter Tingley

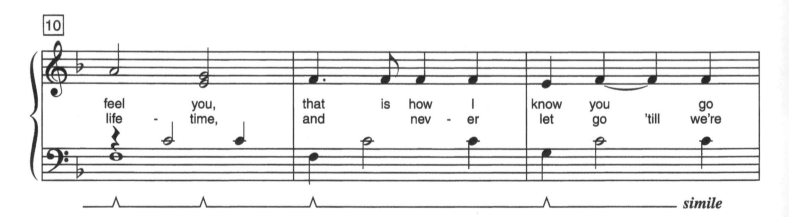

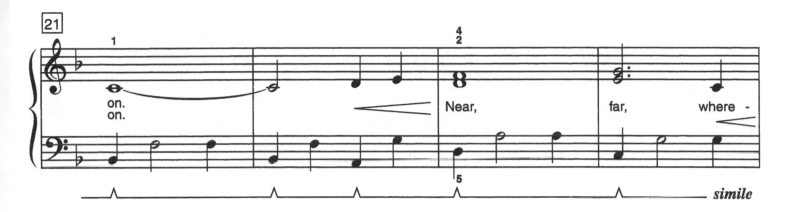

12

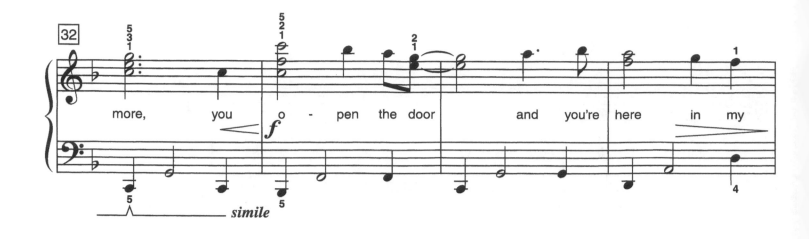

more,   you   o - pen the door   and   you're   in   my

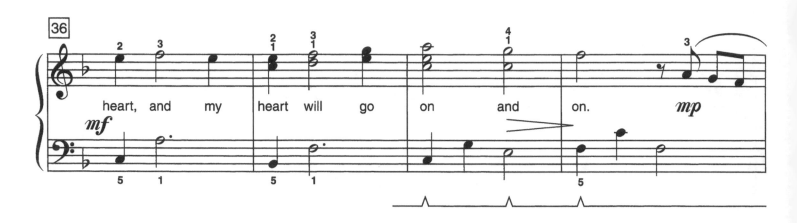

heart, and   my   heart will   go   on   and   on.   *mp*

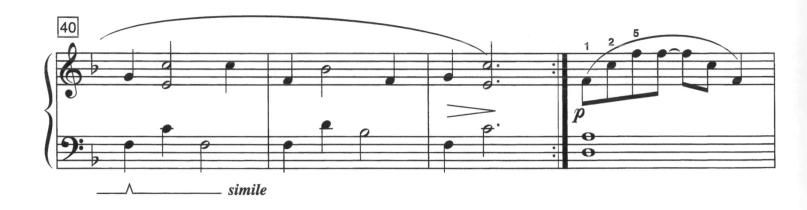

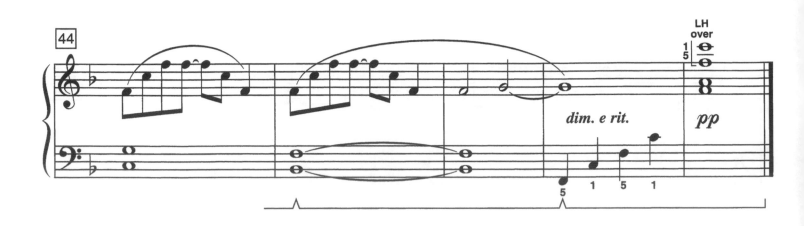

Heart and Soul

from the Paramount Short Subject A SONG IS BORN

Words by Frank Loesser
Music by Hoagy Carmichael
Arr. by Martha Mier

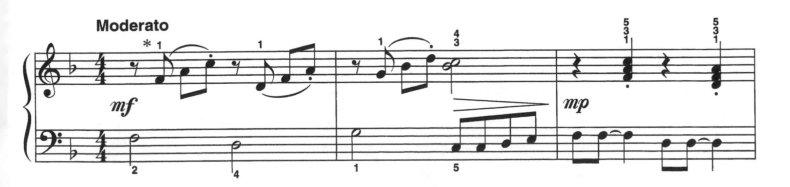

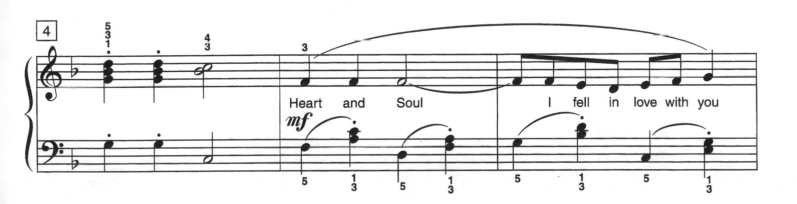

*Optional: Play eighth notes a bit unevenly,
in a "lilting" style: long short long short, *etc.*

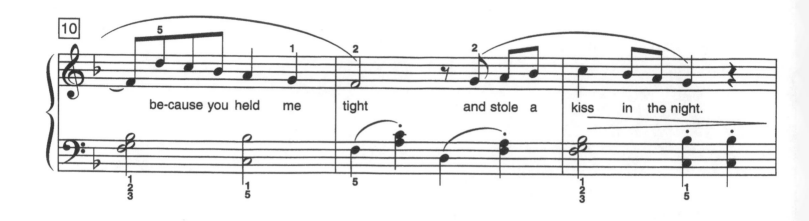

be-cause you held me tight and stole a kiss in the night.

8va

mp

Heart and Soul I begged to be a-dored. Lost con - trol

(8va)

and tum-bled o-ver-board, glad - ly that mag-ic night we kissed there in the

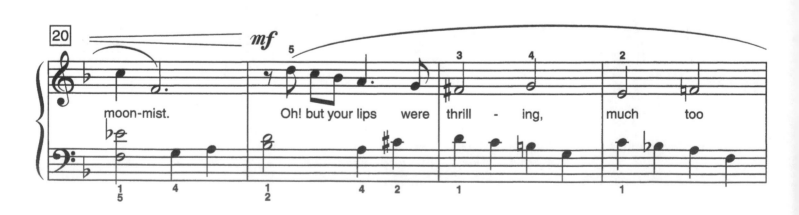

mf

moon-mist. Oh! but your lips were thrill - ing, much too

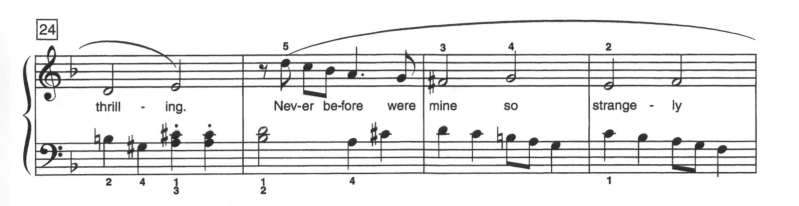

thrill - ing. Nev-er be-fore were mine so strange - ly

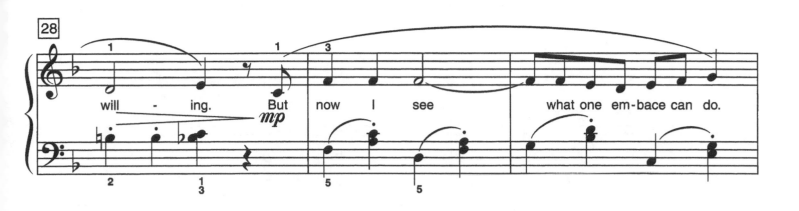

will - ing. But now I see what one em-bace can do.

Look at me, it's got me lov-ing you mad - ly, that lit - tle kiss you

stole held all my Heart and Soul.

A Whole New World

from Walt Disney's ALADDIN

Use after page 27 (57).

Music by Alan Menken
Lyrics by Tim Rice
Arr. by Dennis Alexander

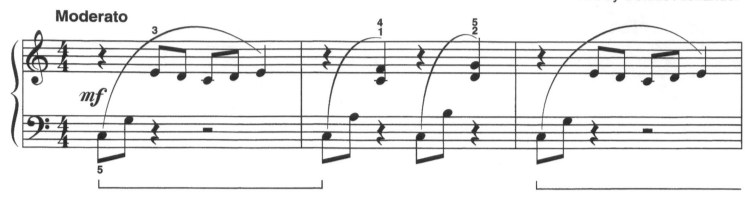

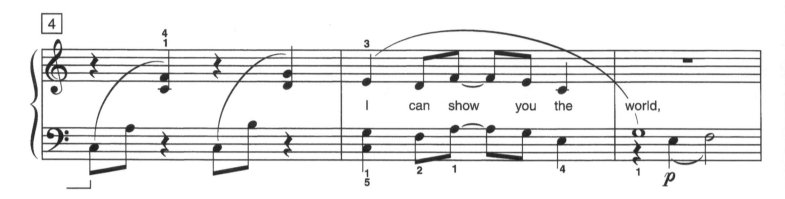

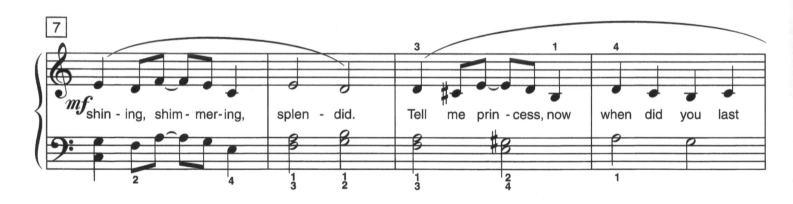

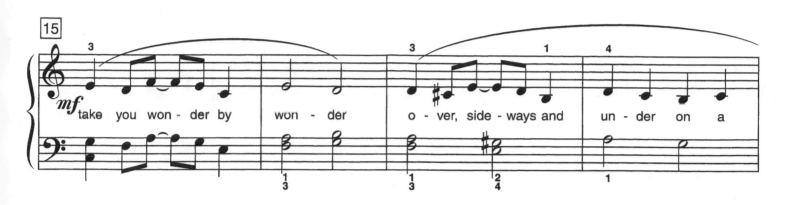

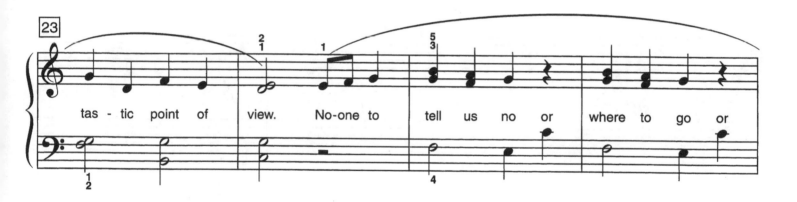

The Sound of Music

from THE SOUND OF MUSIC

Lyrics by Oscar Hammerstein II
Music by Richard Rodgers
Arr. by Sharon Aaronson

*Pedal optional.

Use after page 33 (61).

Colors of the Wind

from Walt Disney's POCAHONTAS

Music by Alan Menken
Lyrics by Stephen Schwartz
Arr. by Christine H. Barden

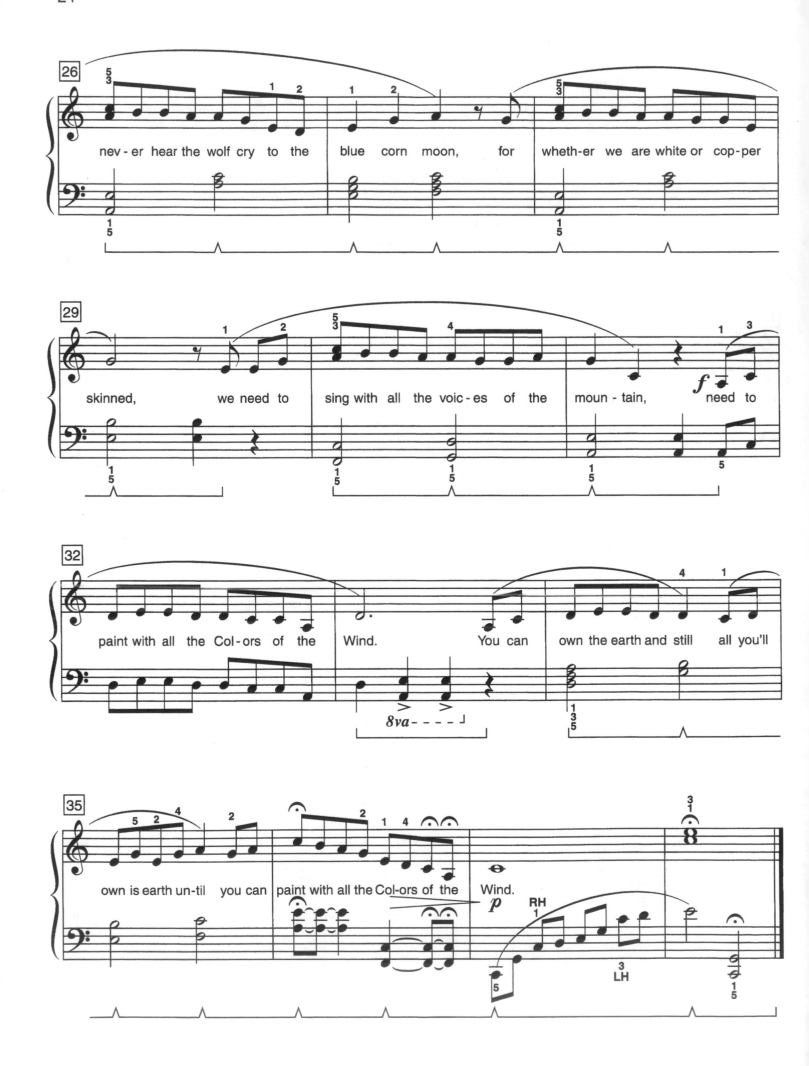

Memory

from CATS

Music by Andrew Lloyd Webber
Text by Trevor Nunn after T. S. Eliot
Arr. by Sharon Aaronson

*Tie 1st time only.

Nadia's Theme

from THE YOUNG AND THE RESTLESS

Use after page 35 (63).

By Barry DeVorzon and Perry Botkin, Jr.
Arr. by Martha Mier

Moderately, with expression

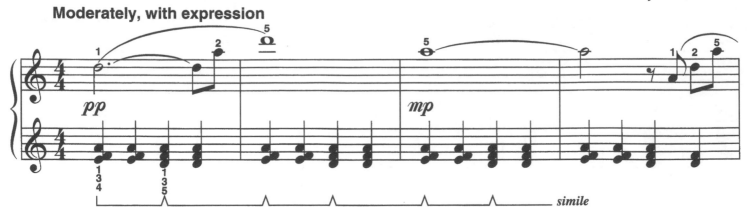

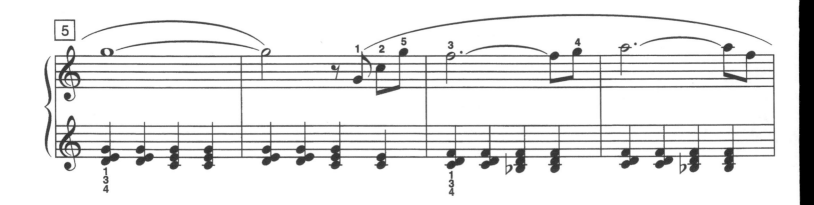

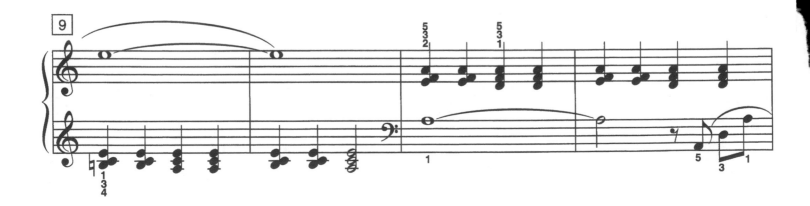

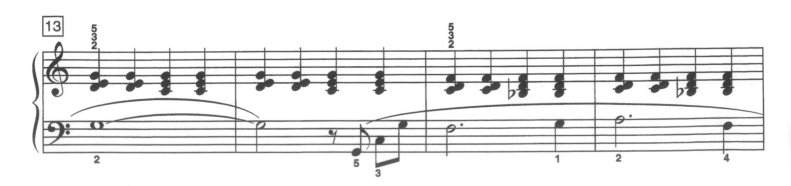

Use after page 45 (71).

Cruella De Vil

from Walt Disney's 101 DALMATIANS

Words and Music by Mel Leven
Arr. by Tom Gerou

17 **2.**
out for Cru - el - la de Vil. *mf* At

21
first you think Cru - el - la is the dev - il, but

25
af - ter time has worn a - way the shock, you

29
come to re - a - lize you've seen her kind of eyes
cresc.

33
f watch - ing you from un - der-neath a rock. *mp* This

vam - pire bat, this in - hu - man beast, she

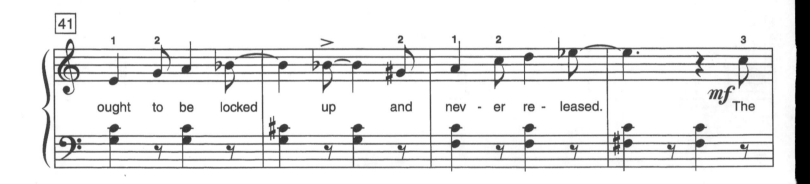

ought to be locked up and nev - er re - leased. *mf* The

world was such a whole - some place un - *f* til Cru -

cresc.

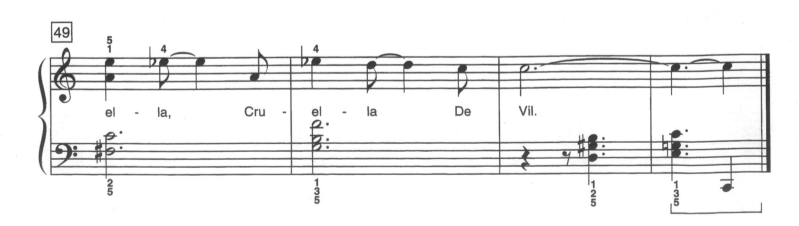

el - la, Cru - el - la De Vil.